MW01258055

# *no idea what I'm doing but f\*ck it*

ron lim

no idea what I'm doing but f*ck it

# chapters

no idea what I'm doing but f*ck it

## what this book is about

I want this book to be something that people can use as motivation to take that little leap out. growing up, we all have a little vision in our mind of what life could potentially be. but as we get older, our dreams get dulled by the standards of society. the vision you used to be so sure about, you are now uncertain. and over time, you start to doubt yourself more and more and you are now unsure if you should ever make that leap. you think there is hope, but you are not so sure anymore. I want this book to help others believe that the "vision" they have is realistic, and not a fantasy. it is there. but just because it's there, it doesn't mean that people are going to get it the moment they reach for it. it just means that it is there. and they can decide what they want to do with that hope. I want this book to be a reassurance for people that it is okay to not know what you are doing. you don't need to know what you are doing. no one knows what they are doing. it is the doing that makes all the difference, not the knowing. I want this book to give people the tiny courage they need to take the next step out. I want this book to be the support for people who feel like they have no support. I want this book to be the living proof that you don't need to know what you are doing to get things done, like me writing this book.

no one knows anything

no one knows anything.

not you. not me. not your parents. not your friends.

but yet we are all stuck in this illusion that
somehow everyone knows everything.

everyone, but you.

and that seems to put you in a bad place. because
now you feel like you are inferior to everyone else.
and you should somehow have known better.

no idea how, but somehow.

the funny thing is – everyone is thinking of the
same thing.

you don't know
what you are doing
so you look for answers
in other people
but the truth is,
nobody really knows
what they are doing either
and instead of letting someone
who has no idea
tell you what to do
why not just fuck it up yourself
anyway?

you disappoint yourself
when you give something
and wait
for the same thing back.

you know.

but you act like you don't.

you want something.

but you talk yourself out of it.

you say it's over.

but you still hold onto it.

you dream of one thing.

but you do another.

and yet, you wonder why you never get there.

a regret:

you can't decide
which choice to go for
so you end up
doing nothing at all.

you say you don't care
but yet you still do
you know the things
you shouldn't do
but yet you still do.

you see yourself
in an endless cycle
with no meaning around
you tell yourself that
you shouldn't stay in it any longer
but yet you still do
another round and round and round.

you don't know
what you are waiting for
so you are just waiting
for something
that isn't going to come.

you're waiting for the right timing.

but are you being logical?

you're waiting for a perfect time – where
everything will work out smoothly.

but there is no perfect time. and the "perfection"
you're waiting for, might not be as perfect as you
think.

there might come a time in the future, where your
problems will become less of a problem.

with enough time, problems sometimes start to
solve themselves.

but is that really perfect?

what about all the time you give up in between,
while waiting for things to be "perfect"?

you want to keep everything, but you can't. you are
afraid to make a wrong decision, so you avoid
doing anything.

you wait for a perfect time, but you end up losing
all the time in between. is that really still perfect?

we hear the most
from the things
people don't say.

if you spend your energy
trying to change things
you can't change
you'd only end up
being depleted
for absolutely no reason.

you say
you want to be special
but yet when you get
an epiphany moment
you choose to ignore it
and be like everyone else.

how many times
have you ignored your intuition
because you were too afraid
of what someone else
might think?

say yes to the things you want to say yes to. we come across opportunities that excite us every now and then. and sometimes we are too passive to say yes, and they are gone before we know it. you can't know if it will work out. but you can't know anything at all if you never say yes to anything.

how different would your life be if you did all the things you told yourself you would?

the energy you spend
worrying about your future
is the same energy you need
to do something
about the present.

no idea what I'm doing but f*ck it

3 things to say yes to:

1. say yes to trying something new. step just an inch out. try something new that doesn't take much of your time and effort. you never know – the new exposure could be what you need to make an eventual shift towards the better.

2. say yes to leaving behind situations that doesn't work anymore. you can't hold onto something that doesn't work or there will never be room for something that does.

3. say yes to reinventing yourself. the whole point of getting new exposure is so that you can make a behavioural shift. if you confine yourself to this "perception" people have of you, then you will always be the same person.

it is the easiest thing
to simply
just do nothing at all
and that is why most people
will not make it.

how many losses
did you take
without even trying
only to find out later that
someone else
has gotten to where you want
by doing the exact same things
you had in mind?

you keep thinking
to yourself
that you are never
going to make it
and that is why
you will never make it.

you manifest
a negative thought
inside you
on repeat
until it comes true
and you call it
*bad luck.*

someone asked me this the other day – "*how do you know what to chase after?*"

and honestly,

you don't.

the truth is – you don't know.

if the thought of something makes you very excited, chase after it.

if there is something you have in mind that you can't stop thinking about, chase after it.

but you never really know what the right answer is.

because there isn't one.

you won't know if it's right, until you have the answer. and you can't get an answer, if you don't try.

honestly, I don't really know what I should chase after either. but you should chase anyway. because that's how you find out.

you wait for others
to point you a direction
and you wonder why
you end up in a place
you don't belong.

are you searching
for an answer
from other people
that only exists
in yourself?

I do not know
where I am meant to be
but I do know
that I do not belong here
and that is enough
for me to leave.

leave if you feel like shit

you gotta start living for yourself. do the things you want to do. come up with new ideas. make changes. just. try. stuff. fuck it up a few times. whatever. you will still be alive anyway.

*leaving*
felt like the most foreign thing
until you are in a foreign place
far away from home
and you realise that home
was never where you want to be
in the first place.

everything is okay.

but I want so much more than okay.

make a change.

and you can always go back to what you've left behind.

chances are, you probably wouldn't want to go back once you make a leap forward. but yet, you spend the vast majority of your energy debating if you should take a leap.

that's the thing about us as humans – we are good at moving forward. we intuitively try to move forward in whatever circumstances we are put in.

when you put yourself in an environment with tremendous upside to grow, you will intuitively figure out a way to get there.

but if you trap yourself in an environment where you are already done growing, then there really isn't anything much left for you to do.

if you're debating to yourself if you should make a change, the answer is yes. you can always go back to what you've left behind.

you've got yourself
and that's all you need
to make a change.

it is better to fuck up
than to live your entire life
and have nothing
happen at all.

there is a kind of tiredness
that sleep doesn't make go away
it comes from the aching of your soul
longing to be someone else
tired of pretending to care about
all the things you don't care about.

there is a kind of tiredness
you cannot make go away
it lays there deep in your soul
growing more and more weary
as you continue to do things
that does not feed your soul.

how many times
do you need
to go back and forth
to make up that decision
you've known all along?

anywhere
is the right direction
if you don't care
where you are going.

if you wait for too long,
it won't be the same
anymore.

at sixteen years old,
fear is not being able to fit in
not funny enough
not skinny enough
not smart enough
not having enough friends
or no one to hang out with
fear is staying at home
when you wanted to be out

at nineteen years old,
fear is leaving your comfort zone
wanting to try something new
but having no one to do it with
and being too afraid to try it alone
fear is having friends say yes
and backing out the last minute

at twenty two years old,
fear is being stuck in the same routine
being in a place you wanted to get out
since you were before sixteen
fear is not trying enough
when you were younger
and probably making the same mistakes
because you are still afraid

at twenty five years old,
fear is being as lost as ever
you're clearly an adult now
why does nothing still make sense?
fear is never being enough
never ending up anywhere
because you don't know where to be
fear is finally trying the ideas
you've always had in your head
and still ending up
in the same old place

what are you more afraid of
is it really change
or things
staying the same?

stop giving your energy to people who make you
feel like shit.

sometimes
the best thing
you can do for yourself
is to leave.

3 things leaving taught me:

1. change is possible. maybe things will suck at the beginning but you will feel happier. and that's better.

2. you're stuck because you're afraid that you will never have it as good as you do now. but that's not true. you've outdone yourself plenty of times before. you can and will do it again.

3. you learn quicker by making mistakes than trying to avoid them. don't overthink. do what you feel is right. if you make a mistake, you can always fix it.

at the end of it all
the biggest obstacle
still remains
to be yourself.

the other day
someone asked me
*how do you make it so easy*
leaving everything behind
and go
just like that.

I thought for a minute
and to that I answered
when you run out of reasons to stay
and your soul is pulling you to go
you would know,
and that
is the time to go.

if there is anything
leaving has taught me
it is that
change is more possible
than we think.

it's better to be lost
than in a place
you don't want to be in.

there will come a time
when it is time to leave
don't rush it
if you are not there yet
you don't need to leave now
but when the time comes,
take a deep breath
and get the fuck out of there.

sometimes
the best self-care thing
you can do for yourself
is to not care.

you break your own heart
by telling yourself
to give it another shot
when you already know
it is time to let go.

you grow older and some things are just not the same anymore.

places that once felt like home could no longer contain your ambition.

people you still have love for but not everyone wants the same things as you do.

you don't have to shrink yourself to fit in places you have outgrown.

life is not meant to live in one area.

make your own mistakes

it only has to make sense to you.

not anybody else.

if it makes you happy, it is a good enough reason to do it.

if you think that it is what you need, it is a good enough reason to do it.

it doesn't matter if others don't agree, they are not you.

make your own mistakes.

what is the one thing you would do if you weren't so afraid?

it's always
the choices
you didn't make
that come back
to haunt you.

give it some time.

stick with the decision you have chosen and just let things play out.

let yourself live through the process.

you don't have to evaluate things right after you make the decision. you won't know it so quickly.

let life happen. and let yourself live for a little.

you gotta get the bad days out. the days you spend sitting on bed wishing you could be elsewhere but there is nowhere else you want to be. the days where creativity just doesn't flow. the days where you try to make plans and they all end up being cancelled. the days where people are just not available and things just don't work out. you gotta get those days out. bad days come and bad days go. it's like going through a deck of cards. you gotta get the bad ones out to make space so you can draw the good ones again.

make your own mistakes,
deal with the consequences
of your own decisions.

people change
just like how you are
no longer the same person
you were two years ago

your past
does not define you
if you fuck up
you can always get back up

some days
feel like years
and sometimes years
can happen in a few days

nothing happens
and then it does
all at once

it's okay
if you change your mind
or do the wrong things twice
you live and you learn
and that's just how it is sometimes

you don't always have to get it right the first time.

there is a certain kind of power that comes with fully accepting your circumstances for what it is. knowing that you can't change the situation in this immediate moment, but it doesn't mean that it will always be this way. knowing that you have the power in you to change things, but it takes time. and if anything, time and effort are two of the things you have in you to give. and understanding that with enough effort and time, you can change anything. it is all within your control.

I've always thought I'd go back
if I ever had the chance to
but I won't
not because I don't want to
because I do,
but I won't

there is a line
between knowing what you want
and what you need
and very often,
they are not the same thing

we make mistakes
and life goes on
we don't always choose right
and life goes on
sometimes we do everything right
still it doesn't work out anyway
and life goes on
and life goes on

isn't it interesting
how we always regret
the things we didn't do
and rarely the ones
we did?

here's a thought.

instead of second guessing if what you did was right, why not just do more?

contemplating about a decision you've made takes energy.

doing more takes energy too.

the difference is that – one is a dead end, the other one is limitless.

often times, you are in control more than you know.

you get to choose where you want to put your energy in.

let yourself flow
towards where
you want to be

life is always flowing
you either flow with it
or you flow against it

neither direction is correct
and neither is wrong
you just want to be flowing
as much as you can

don't make the mistake
of making mistakes
based on
somebody else's terms.

get out.
make mistakes.
do something different.

live the dream
you have always wanted
when you were younger.

the dream that
you have been spending
your whole life
thinking about.

do it once.
it's okay to fail.
it's not about succeeding.
it's about living a dream
you have always wanted.

do it once.
do it before
your life is over.

you are here right now. and you want to be somewhere else. there is a gap between where you are currently, and where you want to be. closing the gap is what motivates me the most.

trying to be
a little comfortable
with the things
that make me uncomfortable
so I can be a little better.

remember, you only fail when you give up.

otherwise, it's only a process of getting there.

it's like you're lost and trying to find the right directions to get to your destination.

you're not a failure for being lost. you just need to find the right direction and then start walking towards it.

at some point
you just gotta take a leap
and live with the consequences
of the decision you made.

some days feel a little
heavier than the rest
but you will always
have time to breathe
and try again.

go where you feel
the most appreciated
or until then,
go figure it out
on your own.

do the things you have in mind.

especially if you have been thinking about it for a long time.

we spend too much time "waiting".

but what are we really waiting for?

waiting till you have a backup plan? waiting for someone to do it with? just simply waiting to see how it goes?

or have you been waiting for so long that you forgot what you are waiting for?

you don't have to do it all at once. take baby steps out.

but don't forget to do the things you have in mind. don't end up waiting in vain.

there is a big world
out there

I want to dedicate this chapter
to tell the story of me leaving
how one thought
led to another
a childhood vision
repeated throughout the years
how I lived my life
looking forward to the day
I get my freedom
my entire existence
leading up to that one singular moment
but still,
I was uncertain
but the thought to not do something
I spent an entire lifetime thinking about
was unbearable
so I had to
for my childhood,
for all the years I wished I was somewhere else
for my future
for myself

*– no idea what I'm doing but fuck it*

pack your bags
buy a one-way ticket
leave
if you feel like shit

all alone
with everywhere to go
but no plans at all,
what should I do next?

it was until I left
that I finally realised
that being away in a foreign place
with no idea of where to go
was actually
what I needed the most.

people seem to think of "the leap" as this
destination that they are chasing.

but in reality, "the leap" is not a destination.

it is not even close to the destination.

"the leap" is the beginning.

it is the beginning of all things new.

you get to decide what you want to be. where you
want to go.

but this time, on your own terms.

homesick
for a home
you are not sure
exists.

make space
for the things
that make your heart
beat a little faster.

I was a child
when I wanted to leave
go live anywhere in the world
I just wanted to get out of here

fourteen year old me
couldn't do shit
didn't know shit
all I knew was that
I didn't want to spend my life in this box
*there is a big world out there*
and I want to see it

the process feels like a long time
when your day to day looks the same
some day I will make it out
life is not meant to live in one place

time takes time
and it's funny when I think about it sometimes
how that one little idea you had
when you were a kid
becomes a part of you when you grow up
permanently

you can spend a long time
wishing for one thing to happen
and when it finally does
make sure you claim it.

but what kind of life is this, really
if I can't do the thing
I want the most.

I'm not sure if it's possible to be fully certain of something you have never done before. I mean – all you have is a vision, right? there is no way you can tell if this vision will come true or not. you can do all the reading, all the talking to people, all the internal debates you have with yourself, and maybe that makes it a little easier. but at the end of the day, you still gotta take that leap. and there is still a possibility that you might hurt yourself in the process. but there will always be that little resistance in you. that little voice in your head telling you that maybe you should reconsider it. but you have already reconsidered it plenty of times. you are trying to wait for that absolute certainty. but deep down, you know that it is not going to come. I think at the end of it all, it comes down to one question – *how much do you really want it?*

I think that makes all the difference.

there is still
so much
left in me
I can't wait to get out.

I think everyone should solo travel at least once in their lives.

3 things I've learned from solo travelling the first time:

1. no matter how much you prepare, there will always be this tiny reluctance to leave. but that tiny reluctance will disappear once you leave.

2. nothing will go completely to plan. nothing. the best plan is to react to whatever comes along.

3. every good thing is momentarily. every bad thing is momentarily. when the travel is over, everything else you did is just a memorable experience. you can't get attached to those moments. but you can always create more memories.

there is hope
in the things
that have not
happened yet.

do it
with all your heart
or don't do it at all.

I've done some things in my life
the same ones people told me
were "too good to be true"
and funny enough,
I think the hardest part of it all
was to convince myself
that I deserved it
and went after the things I wanted
instead of the things I should
and somehow,
that was the biggest contributing factor.

*- self-belief*

you never know
how far you can go
until you decide
to give it a go.

how much
do you actually
want it?

it makes all the difference.

take a step out.

you don't have to do it all at once.

but take one little step. it makes all the difference.

you reach a point in life where you find yourself doing the same things and getting the same results.

same old thing over and over again. and over time, your life starts to come to a standstill.

this is where taking a step out makes all the difference.

it doesn't has to be big. it doesn't has to be significant. it just has to be different. and that tiny difference will be all you need to propel you forward.

the fear of change is not what usually stops you from growing. it is the desire to actually want to move forward. and making the effort to do it.

one little step. by one little step. that's all you need.

how to change your life:

buy a one-way plane ticket

you have come too far
to still be doubting
your own capabilities.

picture this. you're up early and it's quiet outside. the only sounds you hear are birds from too far away, and the cold, crisp air blowing at you. you make a hot cup of coffee and you sit out. it is too cold but you take your blanket outside and you do it anyway. the view is beautiful and the world is calm. inside, you're at peace. there isn't anything else you want to do at the moment. there isn't anywhere else you need to be. you drink your coffee and you think about how just a year ago, where you are now seems like a lifetime away. you are still not where you want to be, not yet. but you no longer feel hopeless and the void that was once inside your heart doesn't seem to be there anymore. you take another sip of coffee. it warms you up from the inside. the trust you have in the process seems to be stronger than ever.

no idea
where I want to be
but I will keep going.

drink more coffee
stay for sunsets
create more,
and fuck things up
a little more often.

who are you
when you are not addicted
by all the internet stimulation

who are you
when you stop doing things
for instant gratification

who are you
when you stop trying so hard
just to get validation

who are you
when no one
is watching you?

all it takes is one.

the answers you need
are in you

pick a direction
and start moving,
the rest will come.

take your own advice.

we have become so good at comforting others.

that we often forget to comfort ourselves when we need it the most.

the advices you need are already in yourself.

listen to yourself.

the answers you need
are really just the same ones,
over and over again.

- *consistency*

you don't know
what you want
but you know
what you don't want
and that is a damn good place
to start.

you gotta embrace your circumstances. you are where you are right now. there is nowhere else you could be in this moment. you can get lost in the idea of where you want to be in the future all you want, but it doesn't change the fact that you are here right now and nowhere else. accept what you can't control. embrace where you are. and keep working on what you know you gotta do to get yourself to where you want to be.

you glow differently when you stop giving a fuck
about what others think.

someone asked me this question the other day:

*do you ever feel like you're wasting time and not actually living, almost like you're waiting to live?*

this is a question I relate to a lot. growing up, I've always felt this way. I've lived my entire life desperately wishing I was somewhere else, doing something else. waiting for my life to start happening.

as I got older, I realised that my life is already happening. it's a mindset thing. waiting is a choice – one that leads to nothing changing.

I couldn't wait anymore. I was desperate for things to change and I wanted it to happen immediately. and it's interesting. because the moment you start to "take control" of the situation, things start to change.

change can happen very quickly. but not always for the better. or at least not immediately. but change is good. especially when you are tired of your constant. any change is good.

embracing change creates opportunities. and opportunities create hope. and hope will bring you the momentum you need to keep going.

the truth is – you are very often more "in control" than you think you are.

make a decision
and the universe
will align
accordingly.

you take the chances
you think you deserve.

if you don't
pick yourself up,
who will?

you've done it once. you can do it again.

whatever you need to get through, you already have it in you.

and you know that.

I know it feels hard sometimes.

you don't know if you want to keep trying. because it feels like you keep ending back up in the same place. so what's the point of trying?

but it won't always be like this.

I can't say better. because I really don't know if there is better.

but I know different. I've seen plenty of different. sometimes they are the same thing. and occasionally, they are not.

it's the hope that keeps us going.

most people will not want
the same things you want
as badly as you
and that is
*your superpower.*

whatever you do,
never forget
your initial intention.

I can't control
what the universe
does to me
but I can control
how I react accordingly

sometimes the universe
throws shit at me
and I go through it
and become a better person

sometimes the universe
throws shit at me
and it hits me flat on my face
and I shrug it off
and walk away
because choosing
to be a bigger person
is easier than dealing with shit
you don't want to deal with

sometimes the universe
throws shit at me
and I simply dodge it.
because I'm not a fucking tree
and I am mobile

but regardless
the universe
does what the universe does
and I am merely
a particle in its entirety

if it's meant to be,
it will come back.

stop telling yourself no.

when your heart says yes.

stop talking yourself out of things you want the most.

you deserve good things.

you deserve to have things you actually want.

let yourself move towards where you want to be.

we tell people
the things we want to hear
but never had the courage
to say it to ourselves
and call it *advice*.

one conversation can change your life.

a concept: just do whatever the fuck you want and feels right. even if it doesn't work out as well as it could if you plan it, you will end up being happier and that's better.

there is so much
we try to say
in the things
we don't say.

you have to believe that things will get better. you have to believe that change is possible. you have to believe that you have the power you need in you, because you do. you have to believe that this path you're working towards will lead to somewhere, and even if you don't get to your end goal right away, you will still be so much further than where you were before.

you have to believe that things will work out, because they will, in due time. you have to believe in the process, because it is as much about commitment and effort as it is about being in the right direction. you have to believe in the possibility of good things happening to you, and accept the losses you have to take along the way. you have to believe that good will come out of it.

you have to believe in yourself. you have to believe that you will be able to figure it out, whatever difficulties you encounter. you have to believe in help. you have to believe in the people who try to help you, and trust that they have the best intentions in their hearts. you have to believe that sometimes people with the best intentions don't end up fitting with one another, and that it's okay if you outgrow them.

you have to just believe – for you make a decision and the universe will always align accordingly. you have to believe that life will always move forward as long as you continue to walk it. you have to believe in the destination and love the process, and believe that while you may not know where you will end up yet, it will be somewhere beautiful.

make your ideas come to life.

remember that one thing you thought you never be able to overcome but you did? yeah. you can do that again.

give yourself time.

whatever that means to you right now.

one day it will come
things will start to work out
and you won't see it coming
because you were too busy
working on yourself.

don't tell me what to do
I don't need your answers
they are not mine,
let me figure out
on my own.

whatever you need, you already have.

you don't need more to get started, you need to start.

the more you do, the luckier you will become.

everything you need to do the things you want is already inside of you.

we all get older
and sometimes we forget
the things we said
we would do for ourselves
when we get older.

growth
is when you look back
at the things you wrote down
when you were younger
and realise
that you don't feel the same
anymore.

maybe
who you are
is all you
will ever need
to become.

no idea what I'm doing but f*ck it

the end

no idea what I'm doing but f*ck it

hello :)

my name is ron. and if you are reading this, it means that I have successfully put together a whole book and figured out how to publish it. I know I will probably feel different about it by the time this book is in your hands, but as of right now in this moment as I'm writing this, the idea of me having a book that I can show to the world feels a little foreign. almost daunting, even.

fun fact – I never wanted nor cared about being a writer. but I did enjoy writing a lot. in the form of tweets in the early days of social media, and Instagram posts throughout recent years. I just never saw it as "writing". all I cared about was that putting all these writings out on the internet was fun, and it made me feel good. so I just kept on at it.

it's funny how life works out sometimes.

if you have read the entire book, I thank you for taking the time. this is the first time I tried writing a book, and doing so was a lot of fun.

I hope I can continue to write more of these.

For more information, please contact:

hello@ronwritings.com

ISBN: 978-981-18-2835-5 (Paperback)
ISBN: 978-981-18-2836-2 (E-book)

Independently Published by Ron Lim

Instagram: @ronwritings

www.ronwritings.com

no idea what I'm doing but f*ck it

no idea what I'm doing but f*ck it